I0074806

20 Toughest Questions on the Internal Audit of ISO 9001 Systems

...and their very practical answers

'Yemi Shodipo

Published by Charis Media

Copyright ©Charis Media

©2015 Charis Media, All Rights Reserved

PREFACE

Sometime in 2014, I sent out a request on the internet asking that audit practitioners ask me their toughest questions on the internal audit of ISO systems. There were quite a number of interesting responses many of them included here; others included were questions raised in the course of consultancy and audit work that were carried out with our clients. I am hopeful that some of the questions here would probably have been asked by yourself at some point and that you will find the answers here practical and capable of moving you forward as an internal auditor and helping you add value to your organisation's quality management system.

This book is not intended to be a project in the theory of auditing; it is intended to ease the way for internal auditors such that the 'massive' things they worry about are made simple for them. It is intended to be the equivalent of being coached by an experienced professional. It is aimed at persons who might have just completed their internal audit training or simply beginning their journey in auditing or the larger field of Quality. I hope you find it a handy companion.

Should you have any comments or additional questions needing an answer I will be glad to respond. Simply contact me on email yemi@charisventures.co.uk

Thanks and enjoy reading "20 Toughest Questions on the Internal Audits of ISO 9001 Systems…..and their very practical answers"

Yemi Shodipo

Consultant

Charis Management Systems

CONTENTS

QUESTION 1

HOW MANY AUDITS SHOULD I CARRY OUT TO MEET THE REQUIREMENTS OF ISO 9001 AND ITS RELEVANT CLAUSE ON INTERNAL AUDITING?

The number of audits required should be as many or as few as reasonably required to cover the below stated requirements of ISO 9001:2008- which defines what the internal audit should cover; 'Planned arrangements', 'ISO 9001:2008' and 'Quality management systems (QMS) requirements established by the organisation'

Working with the assumption that the company's quality management system is properly developed, my understanding is that both planned arrangements and QMS requirements are intrinsically defined in the ISO 9001:2008 quality management system requirements. Therefore an internal audit regime that covers the requirements of ISO 9001:2008 should be sufficient to meet this requirement.

The key factors that determine the frequency of internal audits, in my experience, and I need to stress that the list is not exhaustive, are:

- The size of the organisation and its QMS

- Resource availability (including auditor, auditee and time availability)

- Logistics and other company-specific issues

- Learning from previous internal audit regimes and other system information sources - including non-conformity, customer complaints, customer satisfaction and management reviews.

- Risk thinking

As a rule of thumb, audit frequency should be fit for purpose and make reasonable sense to all parties involved. Carrying out twelve full day audits in a single yearly cycle for an employment agency with only four staff might be considered excessive, based on the business size and potential resource availability.

The number of audits planned should make reasonable sense to the auditor, the auditee, the auditee's manager and the organisation - assuming circumstances are normal and there is no specifically identified imminent risk to the system or organisation. These are the softer factors that determine whether or not an internal audit arrangement will fulfil its intended purpose.

For three different organisations that have the following number of full time equivalent employees – twenty-five, thirty and four. The internal audit arrangements I made were six, six and four half-day audits respectively per annum. It is important to note that these were established businesses with an established management system and there was no evidence in recent years of significant weaknesses in their quality management system. The company with thirty employees initially started off with twelve 'half-days' per year. Over time we discovered that closure of non-conformities were not satisfactorily done by the time the next audit was due, making the next audit begin without having effectively closed out previous findings and many findings were being carried over into the next audit. We reviewed the regime and halved it to six half-days per annum; corrective actions now have the depth and cross functional input that a good system should generate.

Some organisations have a single audit one day audit for the whole year. In my opinion spreading audits across the year allows for continual effectiveness. I once visited a company that planned all its audits during the seasonal downtimes - a key opportunity to probe the system while performing at optimum was lost with this arrangement.

It is generally accepted that a calendar year should represent an audit cycle. I am not aware of any specific requirement in any ISO QMS standard for such, but it is generally accepted and it makes sense, for ease of implementation, review and management.

Whatever number of audits you carry out, whether 1 or 50, all the requirements of ISO 9001:2008 must be covered; establishing conformity, effective implementation and maintenance.

QUESTION 2

HOW CAN I DEVELOP A RISK-BASED INTERNAL AUDIT PROGRAMME?

The internal audit programme/schedule should be based on risk-thinking. Many organisations find it convenient to spread the audits evenly, as this makes the planning activity easier. In good practice systems, the schedule is adjusted to reflect a focus on key areas, either identified as a result of the review of previous audit findings, management review, findings from second and third party audits, or regulatory agencies.

Some of the key factors to consider when putting in place an audit programme or schedule to be reflective of current existing risks of the organisation are as follows:

- Processes that have been known to fail

- Processes that have a regulatory requirement

- Core operational processes

- Processes that have direct impact on customer or other stakeholders

- Processes related to significant findings from data, records and management meetings etc.

- Pre-identified business risks

- Processes that have a direct and significant effect on the bottom line.

If any processes are found to fall within the above, then consideration needs to be made to audit those processes more frequently than ones that are outside these parameters.

I reviewed the internal audit schedule of a client company and discovered that the plan had a provision for auditing operational processes once in a year - the company hired out various categories of equipment (heating, cooling, manual access and powered access equipment). We reviewed the schedule to allow for dedicated and thorough audit of controls related to each group of equipment hired out as this was the company's core process. The volume of business each of these represents could be a further consideration.

As a rule of thumb, remember that the audit programme/schedule should be reviewed and revised as necessary; it is not intended to be a static document year on year.

This is intended to be a simple guidance tool in the operational execution of an internal audit system. Risk based auditing is an extensive topic for which several scholars have produced different works and could be useful further reading.

QUESTION 3

HOW CAN THE INTERNAL AUDIT PROCESS BECOME MORE OF A POSITIVE EXPERIENCE FOR THE AUDITEE?

An internal audit process that covers elements of good practice as identified in this book will help to motivate auditees and employees. Many times the only thing auditees know about the audit process is the auditor himself. I will focus further on the auditor as there are other materials later in the book about audit scheduling, risk based auditing etc. that should all contribute to auditee's motivation.

The following points will contribute significantly towards employee motivation

1. Communication - Before, during and after the audit are key touch points with the auditee. Communicating well before the audit will help pave the way for a smooth flawless audit. No matter how small the organisation is, you must provide the auditee an audit plan ahead of the audit and re-confirm their availability close to the date.

2. Audit as you would like it to be audited. Unless you are one of a few exceptions, nobody likes a know-it-all auditor, who speaks and never listens; who believes he/she wields an authority over people's jobs; who takes delight in driving fear into everyone he speaks to. The auditor should be respectful, engaging, curious and a good listener and not cloud his judgment by preconceived ideas. Stay focused on the evidence.

3. The auditor should be thorough - working through audit trails to effectively close them; take a satisfactory amount of sample to arrive at conclusions; interview a wide range of personnel; take detailed and effective notes. Auditing is an art, doing it well earns the respect of the auditee

4. Value Added Findings - Findings from the audit that appear pedantic and above what can be reasonably expected in an operational environment, only serves to irritate the auditee. Auditors

should recognise that it is possible to audit a system and find no non-conformities on the day. The inability to find non-conformities should not drive an auditor into such findings such as focusing on a grammatical error in a documented procedure for welding on a steelworks shop floor; except, of course, where that error could potentially be interpreted as a wrong instruction.

5. Audits should help to create efficiency, savings and remove bureaucracy. The ability to do this is one of the key characteristics of truly skilled auditors. An auditor whose audit helps to make the auditee's work easier while achieving compliance will have himself a motivated auditee.

6. Auditors should not be negative either in their spoken or written communication- Auditors must recognise that they are part of the organisation's system. They are not inspectors, fault finders; but should have a cooperative approach with auditees. If something is of significance, the auditor should bring it to the attention of the auditee and your feedback should be reflective of the weight of the issue. Simply mentioning something in passing and then raising it as a major non-conformity in the report can be off -putting to auditees and create a negative environment.

7. Remove fear from the audit process. An auditor who can remove the element of fear and put auditees at rest will get the cooperation of auditees.

8. Effective corrective action arrangement. Corrective actions that give clarity of action to the auditee and any required support he/she may need will keep them motivated

9. Quality Management Systems Training/retraining for employees. This will enable employees/auditees to understand the role and purpose of internal audits in the management system and have their questions answered. Retraining at regular intervals could be as pertinent as initial training for some employees.

QUESTION 4

HOW DO YOU COVER THE AREA WHERE AN INTERNAL AUDITOR CANNOT AUDIT HIS OR HER OWN WORK, IF YOU ONLY HAVE ONE AUDITOR?

You need more than one internal auditor for any organisation, with very few exceptions e.g. in microbusinesses, areas with restricted access or other restricting issues; it is always important to have options of internal auditors. I remember establishing a management system in a food manufacturing company that employed about twenty-two personnel; we trained at least five internal auditors to sustain the system.

In many small and medium sized businesses, the quality manager is usually the internal auditor for the whole company. Where this is the case it brings one to question auditor independence on at least parts of the system run by him/her. This conflicts with the expectations of the standard. Where this is the situation additional auditors need to be developed.

Cover in the event of a lack of availability of these personnel.

An option that some businesses use is to outsource parts or all of their internal audit system. Many people think 'outsourcing' internal audits is not acceptable. But the ISO standard that provides guidelines on auditing management systems ISO19011:2011 section 3.1 in its definition of internal audits states the following, 'Internal audits, are conducted by the organisation itself, or on its behalf.

Where the internal audit is commissioned by the organisation to an external party, then as long as the requirements of independence, freedom from bias and conflicts of interest are met, then this is acceptable.

There are other weaknesses that the reliance on a single auditor can bring to the system including in the event of a lack of availability through illness, leaving the business or otherwise, of the only competent internal auditor. This might have implications for your external certification, the effectiveness of the system and control of business risks.

QUESTION 5

DO I NEED INTERNAL AUDITS AS WELL AS EXTERNAL AUDITS? HOW DO THE TWO INTERACT?

This question provides an opportunity to expand on some things outside the traditional understanding of QMS under the ISO 9001 framework and the certification process.

If an organisation has a quality management system (QMS) in place, internal audits are required as part of the support structures to facilitate continual improvement. Whether or not your QMS is externally certified through a regime of third party audits, internal audits need to be carried out. Where organisations have their QMS certified by third party organisations; then an external audit that will usually include an annual audit exercise as a minimum will be put in place.

One of the many unknown things that are clearly detailed in the ISO 9001:2008 standard is the fact that it is possible for an organisation to self-declare compliance to ISO 9001:2008. ISO19011: 2011 goes on to state that 'internal audits can form the basis of an organisation's self-declaration of conformity'.

I recently went to quote for a job for a local small business that has done well over the past few years. Their most significant customer audited them regularly and required that they have in place a quality management system. Whilst they understand the benefits of a QMS, neither they nor their major customer thought a third party certification would be necessary. The normal endpoint of assisting organisations implement a QMS on our quotation format is success at the stage 2 certification audit; for this company we declared a different endpoint; successful completion and closure of findings of a full detailed internal audit against the requirements of ISO 9001:2008.

This is the exception rather than the rule. I am the last person to promote self-declaration of conformity, as I fully understand the basis and reasoning behind third party certification. The importance of effective third party independent review is demonstrated by the standardisation structure that empowers a single body in each country, UKAS in the UK, to accredit bodies that provide third party assessment to the requirements of the ISO 9001 standard. My recommendation – make use of an accredited certification body for the third party certification of your system.

It is important to recognise that there are also unaccredited certification bodies in the market place. Several of my professional colleagues are quick to demonise these organisations; I take a more measured approach. Due to the fact that these organisations are not subject to both the rigours and costs of the (third party) accreditation process, they can potentially provide certification services at reduced cost to businesses. For these organisations to still exist, it tells my business mind that there is a market for them. My position is that if a client chooses to use an unaccredited certification body, they should be fully aware that the body is outside of accreditation control. This can sometimes lead to the non-recognition of that certification by stakeholders who specify accredited certification. I always recommend accredited certification.

Back to the question. The need for the external audits is pedestalled on the accreditation control, which is traceable to established best practice and the prevailing force of law establishing the accrediting body. This assures you that the organisation that provides the third party audit is competent and providing a standardised review of your system. The business world and all the stakeholders you will normally deal with understand and recognise this as verification that you truly have a QMS that meets the requirements of the ISO 9001 standard.

It is impossible to successfully pass through a third party external audit if you have not carried out your internal audit to plan.

QUESTION 6

WE COVER SOME OF THESE PROCESSES AT OUR REVIEW MEETINGS, HOW DO INTERNAL AUDITS DIFFER FROM OUR VARIOUS REVIEW PROCESSES AND INSPECTIONS?

The Oxford dictionary defines a review as 'A formal assessment of something with the intention of instituting change if necessary'.

ISO 19011:2011 defines an audit as 'systematic, independent and documented process for obtaining audit evidence and evaluating it objectively to determine the extent to which the audit criteria are fulfilled'.

The key words in the definition of an audit that are not effectively captured in a 'review' are the words; 'systematic', 'independent', 'documented', 'audit evidence', 'objective evaluation', 'audit criteria' and 'fulfilment'. It is possible for a review to fulfil some of these requirements e.g. documentation and systematic. However, the characteristics of the audit criteria and audit evidence are not fully replicable in the context of a review exercise.

Internal audit is a structured review that has some specified parameters and it is a skill set, and perhaps a profession, that follows a defined set of stages and skills that will provide a predictable result of an effective assessment of the defined process whether or not there are findings from the process.

Dennis R Arter, one of the leading tutors of Internal Quality Audits over the past few decades in a paper on the history of internal quality audits specifies four questions that internal quality audits provide answers to.

1. Have controls been defined?
2. Are the defined controls actually applied by everyone?
3. Do controls really work?
4. Will controls last after the auditors leave?

These questions clearly differentiate an audit from a review. By using the audit tool of sampling, i.e. taking a representative risk based sample of a process/operation, we can review in significant depth that process/operation, making use of various data and information around and about the process/operation to draw conclusions on the four questions above. This skill set is deeper than a review would entail.

Dennis goes on to state that the difference between an audit and an inspection is the fact that an inspection answers the first two questions while an audit answers all four questions.

One of the things that many systems omit is the auditing of the internal audit process itself. In my experience I have seen companies either omit the internal audit process totally from their internal audit programme or simply subject it to a review and deem that adequate. A review in most cases will check that all audits are completed, if there are any findings, whether these have been completed promptly and the status of non-conformity among others.

An audit of the system will, however, establish that the arrangements for internal audits and the corrective action processes for findings are documented, robust and fit for purpose; that the arrangements are consistently carried out at all times without variation from person to person; will question and probe whether existing controls work, whether they could be reviewed for effectiveness, efficiency, ease of use; and obtain objective evidence that the whole arrangement works all year round.

QUESTION 7

PROCEDURES AUDITS VERSUS PROCESS AUDITS. WHICH WOULD YOU RECOMMEND?

Amazingly, six years after the issue of the ISO 9001:2008, a lot of organisations have yet to clearly identify their core processes and the interactions of these processes. Many organisations have a legacy quality management system, where the processes are not clearly identified and the internal audit arrangements structure have remained the same way it has been since the previous two versions of the ISO standard. So what you see is that they have internal audits equal to the number of procedures they have in place. And those internal audits are carried out as per each procedure, probably once a month and they create checklists that are in line with these procedures.

The problem is not in itself having a checklist in line with the procedure; however, the key weakness of this approach is that it looks at the procedure, potentially in isolation from all the other processes or parts of processes that the particular procedure has an impact on.

One of the most important skills that an internal auditor needs is the ability to work through flow charts or process flow diagrams. Flow charts help to gain better understanding of the operations from beginning to end. In the absence of a flow chart, an internal auditor must be able to draw a simple flow chart to help understand the flow of the operations or process being reviewing.

One of the ways in which I describe a process is very simple. If you draw a flowchart of all the actions it takes you to get out of a car to getting seated in the office at 9 AM Monday. You would start the process with you turning off the car engine and then follow this with, placing your hand on the door; opening the door; stepping out of the door; shutting the door back, using the keys to lock the door; turning back and walking away from the car, getting to the entrance of your office etc. Now look at each of those actions from top to bottom, from car to entering the office, and you will see they develop a visual representation of that single activity and this example is one of the best ways to understand processes.

Another example might be a customer order process from beginning to the end: how does the customer trigger an order to how we deliver that order. When you have the steps on a process flow you can then consider what resources are required to deliver the customer order; is the infrastructure required in place; is documentation established and adequate; have key performances been established; is data analysis in place; are competent personnel in place. You can look at all the ramifications as you follow the process from beginning to the end.

When creating a standard process flow chart you could take a sample of previous orders processed and thinking through all the ramifications involved in completing that process.

This understanding will enable you to question the auditee, for example, on what type of training this particular person responsible for a part of the process, has; i.e. 'can I see the evidence that this person has this particular training?' What equipment is required to carry out this particular process; what arrangements do you have for the maintenance of those equipment; if measuring and monitoring equipment is used – is there evidence of the calibration status of that measuring and monitoring. So you begin to see that from a single process you can easily follow that through and consider the requirements based on your knowledge of the standards or company operations and procedures, and you can explore the various ramifications of the process.

You will need to have a good knowledge of the requirements of the quality standards; ISO 9001. As a rule of thumb simply think, 'what can possibly go wrong that can have an effect on quality of product or service', and with probing questions gain assurance that the particular opportunities for things to go wrong have been taken, controlled or where possible eliminated from the process.

The best auditors in my opinion use a combination of process and procedures based auditing.

QUESTION 8

HOW CAN I IMPROVE MY COMMUNICATION SKILLS WITH THE AUDITEE DURING THE AUDIT?

The origin of the word audit is the Latin word 'audire' which means 'hear' or 'hearing'. It is the same root word that produced the English word audio, which of course represents information that can be heard. I think that listening is a skill that auditors must have and use effectively. The more effectively you can listen and observe and be genuinely curious about understanding what the auditee is telling you. Effective listening skills includes both verbal and non verbal communication and so if you understand this then the better you will be at communicating with others.

When we deliver auditing courses we undertake mock audits, and during these activities the recurring theme for these trainee auditors is always their ability to balance listening, observation and note taking whilst planning the next question and following an effective audit trail - all at the same time.

As I write this chapter, I have just finished delivering an Internal Auditor training course at the Chamber of Commerce in Blackpool, UK and it was exactly the same; while the mock audits were going on with myself acting as auditee, I ensured that I said things which would give the students clues as to issues that potentially would be non-conformities in the system; sometimes they picked up these clues, at other times they were too busy either taking notes, reviewing documents or simply hearing and not listening because their minds are focused on the next question.

It might help new auditors to note that even the most experienced auditors do not get it right every time but it should become easier as you become more experienced in your audits and you improve your skills. If you can achieve 100% focus each time you audit while managing all variables you would be doing extremely well. But make sure you do not miss critical or very important parts of the process being discussed.

The better you listen, the better you will be able to formulate and ask more probing questions. I must say at this stage that this skill comes with continued practice. The more you practice the less pressure you will feel when planning the next question, and be able to focus on gaining insight from the answers you are being given.

Every auditor benefits from having a checklist and even the most experienced auditors still keep some kind of checklist, no matter how scant. This couldsimply be the audit plan; detailing the areas to be checked. It is a checklist of some sort as it reminds them what to look at.

There are also many different types of auditees, some will ramble on and on, some have been told to say the minimum possible, some find your audit an interruption from their already difficult day's work and are glad to be rid of you and yes some can be extremely uncooperative and even rude. If you remember that your job is to understand what the auditee does and assure yourself that the operations meets the audit criteria to which you are working; whether this be ISO 9001 itself or a company procedure, customer requirement etc. You should focus on, and do whatever you need to do to obtain that information while remaining professional at all times, regardless of the reception you get.

As a rule of thumb, I think people positively respond to someone with a keen sense of curiosity, respect for what the auditee does, humility and ease of approach. A know-it-all, condescending, fault-finding policing-type enquiry will usually result in auditees being less responsive in providing the information you need for a successful audit.

QUESTION 9

IT IS SAID THAT AN AUDITOR SHOULD BE 'FLEXIBLE'. DOES THIS MEAN THAT WE SHOULD BE INCONSISTENT, APPLYING THE RULE THOROUGHLY IN ONE AREA AND LESS SO IN OTHERS?

Let me start out with this rather far-fetched example when I was training to be an auditor.

I was with a company with an international presence and sent as part of the internal audit team to audit company operations in China. The China operation was a joint venture business with our company. I was still a trainee auditor at this stage and had a very experienced lead auditor.

During the audit, I picked up a number of issues, which, as a good auditor should do, I mentioned to the auditee at the time that these would be a problem. As I closed my audit, (and I should not have done this before clarifying with the lead auditor), I told him the seven findings I had. He suddenly became very defensive, arguing every point he had previously agreed and I was genuinely taken by surprise and the lead auditor had to intervene.

I would later realise, on my return to the UK that the existing culture with his employers and our joint venture partners was that his salary was deducted for every single finding that came out of his department. Now that's tough! Unfortunately there was no way I could have had known that situation before beginning the audit.

Like I said that is an extreme example; but it might be useful to have some brief foreknowledge of whether the department you are reviewing has a blame culture established in it and that your findings will be interpreted as individual failures.

You might be interviewing personnel who are currently serving the consultation time of their redundancy period; perhaps not the best person to interview for many reasons. It is also useful to understand what is specifically within the control of the area/people you are auditing and not assume anything.

Because the primary duty of an auditor is to obtain evidence of conformity to the audit criteria e.g. ISO 9001, being flexible as a person will help you obtain the evidence you require accurately.

21

For example, you are auditing a high-pressure production line and the line manager has insisted your audit be postponed. You have the option of insisting that they cooperate with your audit or you might speak to the line lead/supervisor and ask 'what time within the next week is actually best for me to carry out the audit with you people?'

If your aim is to carry out an effective assessment; I would suggest that the second approach would be the better approach. But if your aim is to wield your power as an auditor, you might insist on proceeding with the audit at the time; but get the least cooperation possible from the team. Bottom line is your audit was less effective because of your rigid approach.

Auditing is a people function. There is unfortunately, the existing perception of auditors being some kind of enforcer! No. An auditor is simply an evidence seeker and is only successful when he gets appropriate evidence. Does this mean that only people-persons should become auditors? No. I believe the people skills required for internal auditing can be learned; just like any other skill.

QUESTION 10

I HAVE A PROBLEM WITH MAKING A JUDGEMENT ON THE CATEGORISATION OF NON-CONFORMITIES. WHAT MAKES NON-CONFORMITY IN THE FIRST PLACE? AND WHAT IS THE DIFFERENCE BETWEEN A MAJOR AND A MINOR NON-CONFORMITY?

When a stated requirement is not fulfilled, you have non-conformity! Whether that requirement is stated in the ISO standard or company policy, procedures, work instruction or other documents in the organisation.

ISO defines non-conformity simply as 'non-fulfilment of a requirement'. So where the standard says, for example, 'a documented procedure shall be established....' and there is no documented non-conformance procedure; that is non-conformity. In the standard 7.5.1a it states that there is a requirement for the availability of 'information that describes the characteristics of the product', and if the auditee is unable to provide either a product description, a product specification document, product catalogues or similar other evidence and simply explains that our customers know our products; this is a non-conformity.

Will this definition apply even if it is only one product affected in your example quoting clause 7.5.1a? The answer is YES! It is an unfulfilled requirement and more so at the level of an internal audit. The internal audit by design is expected to be more thorough and more detailed than the few days snapshot that external auditors have of a company's system.

Let it be established here that a company could choose to interpret and establish what it considers to be the definition of non-conformity in its own context. But for those who seek guidance, the ISO documents describe it as above.

Some organisations might choose to go ahead and further classify the non-conformity either as a major non-conformity or a minor non-conformity. I believe it is the third party certification bodies that popularised this classification and use it the most. I will, therefore, use a similar guidance to the one used by these bodies.

A minor non-conformity is a non-fulfilment of requirement (Same definition as non-conformity); a major non-conformity, however, is

23

essentially a breakdown in the effectiveness of a process or system. For example in the cases above; let us suppose there are numerous occurrences where ISO required documented procedures i.e. for control of documents, control of records, internal audit, non-conformity, corrective action and preventive action. Three or more of these mandatory documents are not in place therefore there is a case for a major non-conformity. In a second scenario: if the company made about twenty products and there are no clearly defined product characteristics for, say, five of the products, then there is a case for a major non-conformity.

This is because, in these examples, it goes beyond the requirement not being met; there is evidence that the process that ensures the meeting of that requirement is NOT reliable enough to ensure that requirement of the standard is consistently met.

I trust these examples help put it in some perspective for internal auditing purposes. Third party auditors sometimes use greater flexibility in this judgment and may interpret a process breakdown as something that does not fulfil a range of requirements rather than just one requirement.

It is important to note, however, that ISO does not appear to have, in any of its documents, a definition for the terms major and minor non-conformities; it only talks of non-conformities. Bottom line is that the organisation needs to decide what works best for it.

Sometimes organisations also use the expression 'observation'. This is used to refer to things that might not be non-conformities at the time of the audit; but in the auditor's judgement requires a review. These are usually advisory. E.g. The technician might benefit from a refresher course considering the gap between the last time he was trained; or efficiency advice e.g. consideration for customer relationship management software might assist in reducing dependence on a significant number of spreadsheets.

QUESTION 11

HOW DO YOU AUDIT 'MANAGEMENT COMMITMENT / LEADERSHIP'?

When people ask me this question, I realise that what they are really asking is 'how do you carry out an audit 'interview' of senior management?'

While interviewing is a key auditing skill, I will start by mentioning a key approach I use in carrying out an audit of management commitment. I use the interview with senior management or their representatives to cap up my audit of management commitment.

My first rule of thumb is to ensure that management commitment is one of the last things, if not the very last thing I will audit on my audit schedule or audit plan as may be appropriate. This enables me to have audited most parts of the management system and get a feel for how committed the leadership is in providing resources, support, engaging with and championing the management system.

I review whatever findings I may have had, and whatever objective evidence I may have seen that either supports or demonstrates a lack of management commitment. The suitability of facilities, tools, materials and finished products; availability of key requirements that support the system, e.g. calibration arrangements, clear structured customer complaints system that leads to clear root cause evaluation and communication back to the complainant; industry best practice training for staff and any relevant excuses given in the event where staff training is not up to industry standard etc. These findings, good or bad, form the agenda of my interview with the senior management. In putting these to senior management across a table, I am checking for:

1. A clear awareness of what is going on in the company management system

2. What is happening, positive or negative; is it by their design or simply a consequence of the system or lack of system they have put in place

3. An understanding of the implications of positive and negative findings; are they simply dismissive of clear concerns

4. A structured approach to resolving any findings

5. An openness and willingness to engage in discussion about any thorny issues

6. Gauging and measuring the point between resource constraints and resource as an excuse

7. An understanding of how components or the entirety of their management system, directly links to the company's business competitiveness and their supply chain assurance

8. Engagement with the system

I do stress here that many of the things gained from the interview will be subjective rather than objective evidence, but the discussions from the interview will shine a light on the objective evidence you have previously obtained.

An auditor has to resist the temptation to raise non-conformity on management commitment simply based on the interview with senior managers as the outcome of these might be difficult to manage. Sometimes it takes several audits before we have tangible evidence to suspect inadequate management commitment, before we can identify the objective evidence that fully demonstrates that management commitment is lacking or inadequate.

Until we get that objective evidence we do not raise non-conformity on management commitment. We may express our concerns as observations or even include such concerns in the executive summary; this is true for management commitment as it is true for any other findings from an audit.

The weakness of interview as a source of objective evidence is what makes me advocate viewing the audit of management commitment as what it is; a larger exercise than the narrow issue of 'senior management audit interview'. In fact in some ways, the whole internal audit exercise is an audit of management commitment. It (the interview) must be done, but the outcome needs to be put into context.

Auditors also need to be sensitive to the political, business and any other prevailing interests in their organisation, which potentially could come to a head when the opinion or positioning of senior management is brought to discussion at a senior management audit interview. Any auditor who is dismissed or disciplined for the manner of questioning or audit findings they raised in an internal audit, in most reasonable environments, has clearly not demonstrated the emotional intelligence required to do an internal auditor's job effectively. There needs to be a balance between being sensitive to the organisational culture and being firm and remaining objective.

QUESTION 12

HOW INVOLVED SHOULD THE INTERNAL AUDITOR BE IN THE IMPLEMENTATION OF CORRECTIVE ACTIONS?

An internal auditor is 'internal' to the company. He or she is part of the company and, therefore, depending on the company structure could be involved in the implementation of suitable corrective actions to the findings raised to varying levels depending on the organisation.

In keeping with the principle of independence, I would advise that in the case of internal audits, the auditor can provide guidance to the auditees or manager of the audited sections as to how corrective action should be carried out. Final responsibility and actual delivery of corrective actions, I would advise, remains with the process owner or manager. The auditor should be careful not to be drawn into undertaking the corrective action process, as there is a danger of losing objectivity. So whilst I would be happy to provide guidance, even detailed guidance, I would leave the process operatives to correct the

process root causes; this of course is assuming some level of competence in the corrective action process of either the operative or the operative's manager as a minimum (this should be safe to expect of an ISO 9001 certified organisation).

I consider the internal audit process to, in itself, be an internal consultancy process; which is a major differentiating factor from the second or third party audit assessment. Independence from the job function must always be maintained, but responsibility for action on non-conformities, whilst this lies with the process manager, the internal auditor could potentially share parts of this responsibility to a lesser or greater degree, depending on how the company's corrective action process is set up. If, however, the auditor is convinced that involvement at any level will compromise his/her independence and the organisation is resourced enough then the auditor could stay completely independent of the corrective action process as, say, a third party auditor would do.

Where the organisation is extremely limited in resources though, while the process manager still bears the final responsibility for the corrective action, there is no ISO requirement demanding independence of personnel carrying out the corrective action process and so it is not technically wrong; but may not be in the best interests of keeping with the spirit of the standard. In such situations, the internal auditor could be hands-on in

27

the corrective action process and still be in a position to close out the finding (however this is not the spirit in which the standard is intended).

QUESTION 13

WHAT IS THE BEST TRAINING / QUALIFICATION PROCESS YOU RECOMMEND TO BECOME A GOOD INTERNAL AUDITOR?

At the risk of being controversial, the ISO 9001:2008 standard does not require structured 'training' to carry out any task within the quality management system. The section 6.2.2 which is subtitled Competence - training and awareness - and its sub points actually shows us that the standard is more concerned about competence. However, it recognises training as one of the ways to achieve the required competencies for roles. Organisations, however, have a duty to identify and demonstrate best practice as defined by their industry requirements and standards, so where there is specific training identified within the laws or industry good practice, it is expected that good organisations will adopt this.

Bringing this back to the internal auditor; the requirement is that the internal auditors will be 'competent'. Structured internal auditor training could be one of the easiest ways to start building this competence. I remember attending the Lead Auditor Course for ISO 9001 but still lacking confidence in carting out an effective audit of an ISO 9001 system. This is because, whilst I had been trained, I was not yet competent having had little or no experience.

Now I feel competent and the difference between now and then is that I have shadowed numerous audits by experienced auditors. I have been mentored and have had my questions answered, I have practiced my auditing skills under the experienced eyes of the audit mentors and I have been through a process of auditor examinations based on live audit performance called 'witness auditing'. In a witness audit, an experienced auditor watches you perform a full audit and prepares a report on your audit and concludes whether or not you have demonstrated the required competence on the day. It is amazing how many people walk out after the training examination, get a pass result and declare themselves competent.

In spite of the comments above, I still advocate attendance at an internal auditor course, as it serves the purpose of providing a good grounding of knowledge on what is required of an internal auditor. In the UK, IRCA (International Register of Certificated Auditors) runs approved 2 day Internal Auditor Courses and is considered the Gold Standard. Although there is a mock audit session during the training, in my opinion and that of other knowledgeable practitioners in the auditing profession, we believe that this is inadequate in itself to declare a person competent!

This is why third party certification bodies, auditor training and qualification processes, requires several days of audit shadow, audit team memberships and lead audit function including a witness audit as part of the competence requirement and assessment processes.

I would state that the best internal auditor competence process will involve over and above internal audit training. As a minimum, shadowed audits, auditor mentoring and some form of observed/witness audits. This process should be carried out involving a range of different company processes. Individuals can trial it with several processes in their organisation over a concentrated period of time, say three months. The outcome should be a confident internal auditor who is able to deliver value-adding findings to the organisation.

QUESTIONS 14

DOES RISK THINKING BRING INTERNAL AUDITS INTO THE REALM OF THE SUBJECTIVE?

This question was asked at an event we organised to inform businesses in the North West of the UK on the expected changes to be introduced in the ISO 9001:2015 standard. A concerned business owner, wanted to know what would happen on an audit if the risk judgement of the company significantly differs from the risk judgement of the auditor.

Let's take an example: A logistics company carrying hazardous waste. The company might deem it unnecessary to secure the waste tanker with a traceable seal identification system as one would expect in, say, a bulk haulage company involved in the food industry. The auditor might think they need to demonstrate the same level of security controls. Who is right and who is wrong?

The answer is not straightforward, but it raises the new skills that auditors and many personnel involved in management systems will need to acquire to effectively fulfil the risk thinking focus of the new standards. Firstly internal auditors need to have some level of risk management training, to enable them make risk judgements that are relatively calibrated with good practice. I personally believe that auditors without risk management competencies will be significantly handicapped under the new version of ISO 9001.

A good auditor will, however, listen intently to the reasons why and how the risk judgement was arrived at. It is best if this risk judgement is documented, but it will not be uncommon to come across risk judgements that are not documented especially if it is not part of the core risk of the organisation.

The new ISO standard does not require specific documentation as did the previous standard and an auditor's job will be to establish if the risk has been thought through, established and communicated, at least with and by the personnel that will have the most responsibility for managing that perceived risk. Auditors might have to move further towards a less mentioned part of our job, which is to ESTABLISH CONFIDENCE in the arrangement, systems and risk judgement that are in place. If the auditor is not confident in the arrangements in place, it is important that this lack of confidence is communicated in some way. I make good use of the tool of 'observation' or inclusion in the executive summary if I am not as confident in a process as I would like to be; but do not have adequate objective evidence to establish that the process is not compliant to the requirements of the standard. However, if you can find objective evidence, perhaps in cases where the tanker content was compromised en-route, then you have your objective evidence of the inadequacy of the risk based controls.

In some ways internal audit makes use of objective evidence to draw subjective conclusions. E.g. I chose five job samples and three of the jobs were not clearly traceable through the work flow. The clear details of the jobs, the job number, dates, customer involved, actual description of the job etc., is the objective evidence. My subjective conclusion is that 'the arrangements for the traceability of jobs through the system, does not appear to be consistently effective based on the samples reviewed'.

So there is always an element of subjectivity in an audit. The best audits will make 'subjective' conclusions based on 'objective' evidence. Risk based auditing should not negate this fundamental principle.

QUESTION 15

IS IT POSSIBLE TO HAVE NO NON-CONFORMITY OVER SEVERAL AUDITS?

It is possible to audit a management system and find no non-conformity. Not finding non-conformity does not suggest a management system is perfect but is based on an audit that was carried out on a day, where there was no non-conformity found. This is perfectly normal but if the organisation has had a long history, running into years of no non-conformities in the internal audits, then it might be a cause for concern. This is because it would suggest that the management system is perfect, which is impossible, it can be near perfect but not perfect. There are a few reasons why you would have no non-conformities for long periods of time but it is usually down to one root cause.

1. It could be that the auditor is not skilled enough in the auditing process. This is the ability to probe into an existing management system, ask questions, seek objective evidence and establish confidence in that particular process.

2. Maybe detailed information is not probed enough. Sometimes we can just audit on the surface or have an auditee that provides surface information. It is important to dig deep into a process to get down to any underlying issues that may exist.

3. When people carry out audits without the use of sampling. Sampling is a very powerful tool used in auditing, which picks at random potential evidences that can help to establish confidence. If you do not thoroughly check risk based, risk judged samples of evidence, there is the possibility that the auditee could provide you with prepared evidence for you to work with, or you might take what is stated in a document and, therefore, establish that it conforms. Before you establish conformity you should look at a range of documents, otherwise the sampling is not done properly.

4. Sometimes an auditor may pick up non-conformities and not document it for a variety of reasons. If non-conformities are not documented it helps no-one, not the auditor, not the management system nor the auditee. This is because, what is not documented cannot be followed up on, so we cannot be certain that the appropriate corrective action is carried out or that we have learned from that corrective action to prevent the issue from reoccurring.

5. Another area critical to this can be the culture of the organisation. I heard of an organisation where, as part of the job description of the quality manager, it said that there should not be any non-conformity in

internal and external audits. This means that although there would be no non-conformities documented, for success in the job, it does not always mean there are no non-conformities in the system. It is very important that the culture of the organisation is supportive and willing to accept non-conformities and addressing or dealing with any non-conformity appropriately.

6. In some organisations the role of an internal auditor is not understood. Some just understand it as a tick box exercise that has to be done and, therefore, have no expectations that any findings or actions will result from the audit.

All these things can lead to not having non-conformities raised at audits when there actually might be some in the system for extended periods of time. The core thing is to have an auditor that knows his job and is well skilled within it. A competent auditor not just trained but who is competent by virtue of training and experience. Having this kind of auditor is the key way to address the issue long term non-conformities not being raised on a long term basis.

QUESTION 16

HOW DO YOU CARRY OUT SAMPLING?

Throughout these write-ups I have placed considerable emphasis on sampling. Sampling is just as simple as it sounds; it is simply taking a sample.

It needs to be understood that an auditor is not someone with power and influence coming into your business to declare what is good and what is bad. It is someone coming to find objective evidence that suggests that a particular management system complies with the audit criteria, whether it is ISO9001 or company procedures.

For the auditor to come to that judgement, whether it be document control, manufacturing process or service delivery process, etc. they will want to take a few samples, as randomly as possible, to look through in relative detail to satisfy the auditor that what they can see of the samples of this system or process can be relied on to consistently deliver what is expected of it.

If we look at a manufacturing process, let us say the process starts from goods inwards to goods outwards, and we want to audit this process. Sometimes I will look at the process from the end, from the finished products, and try to work through all the steps backwards as described in the flow diagrams.

In good companies, along with the flow diagrams, they will have an equivalent quality plan. If not, I will look at the flow diagrams and make a judgement on where the quality points are, where it is critical for the product or service to be delivered effectively. This enables you to look back at all the quality points and all the places where they say that document and data will be captured to verify that things are being done properly.

You can work backwards or forwards from beginning to end. With sampling, once you understand that process you will take, for example, things that were manufactured over that last five months. For instance, ask for an example of widgets that have been manufactured in particular months, or two orders for biggest customer. Then pick those at random and establish that each time quality checks are being carried out, quality requirements are being fulfilled all across the process from goods in to goods out. For a simpler example let's look at training. Rather than asking for what they have for training, you might have identified the individual who works in the warehouse, the person who handles the customer order process, the person in charge of inspection, and from these you select a range of these employees.

Once selected you look into their records to check for any training the individuals have undertaken. For example, with the individual who works in the warehouse driving a forklift? Does he have a forklift driving license? Has he been through an induction? Has he had some basic health and safety training? What particular skills would you expect him to demonstrate his competence? And you would ask for evidence to see how that competence has been put in place. You would do this for five or six employees and if they are all good then you are in a good position to establish confidence based on the sample that you have chosen.

You can go into a company and they have had a hundred non-conformities through the year. You would not look at all the one hundred non-conformities, but you can use various criteria based on your judgement to select a range of non-conformities. It might be the ones that are internal, that are selected for one department. Or you might choose to select the ones where the findings are due to human error or findings are as a result of machine error. Select all of these and put them together.

Look at the procedure for dealing with non-conformities and verify with the five or six non-conformities which you have selected where that procedure is followed. Where procedures are not followed from the samples you have selected, a non conformity exists. This approach helps the company gain confidence that the process is always carried out in the same way all the time.

You may come across cases where it is just impossible to sample, where there is only one particular document or one particular record. Where the organisation needs a particular license or similar to function and you want to verify that, they only provide you that single license information, therefore, sampling will not work. It is a case of using common sense, but you put down in your audit report the objective evidence of the particular license, the license number, the date issued and the authority it is issued by, as your objective evidence. Wherever possible do try to get a sample to establish confidence in a process, it is fundamental to the skill set of auditing both internal and external.

QUESTION 17

WHEN PEOPLE REACT UNFAVOURABLY TO NON-CONFORMITIES RAISED AGAINST THEM, HOW DO I DEAL WITH THIS?

I would like to start by saying that auditors should *not* raise non-conformities against *people*. We raise non-conformities against processes and systems, not people. If your audit simply looks out for human error issues and catalogues it in a report, then you will make more enemies than you need to because everyone will do their best to avoid the tag of a 'bad employee' in the workplace.

I have seen internal audits where there is provision for detailing 'person at fault'. Such things can only foster a blame culture; it is only in very few occurrences that issues are caused by the person. Fault is more likely to lie with the system that was set up to get the task/process done.

I recently audited a system and looked at the records for a particular customer complaint which showed that a part manufactured by the customer was made with the wrong material. The root cause identified was 'operative error'. I was not convinced. For a part to go out made from the wrong material due to only one operator's error, in a company that employs over sixty people and carries out several processes was a near impossible feat. And so I questioned further, interviewed and looked at records again. We discovered that, not only for this particular customer complaint, but for much of the manufacturing process, it was impossible to verify that the planned independent first-off inspections by the responsible supervisors were taking place all the time. We also found that the 'final inspection' as detailed in the company procedures was not taking place at all. These would have been two significant opportunities for capturing this issue that later became a customer complaint.

I raised a non-conformity regarding the inspection processes, first-off and final inspections, and the production leadership had to admit that there was no structured final inspection process actually happening on the production floor. This, in my opinion, is an example of an audit adding value – if I do say so myself!

I recognise that there is the argument of building quality, rather than just inspecting it at the final stage. Although the final stage is the best place for a final inspection, getting to that place requires a robust and effective quality assurance and management system in order to reduce the inspection controls at the end. This company, however, had a ratio of 10 customer complaints for every 1 non-conformity raised in-house; which was a pointer to the fact that the in-house ability for the quality system to identify issues and correct itself prior to products leaving the site was exceptionally weak, to say the least.

When we hold people responsible for findings then it can become counterproductive. It could be the equipment, it could be the measuring instrument, it could be the procedure used, it could be the materials involved, it could be the environment or it could be the previous or later processes that account for the bulk of the issues raised against an operative. Usually, if you have a finding where the root cause is a straight forward 'human error' situation, I would suggest that at that stage you have only scratched the surface of the issue, and if you raise a non-conformity at that point you have probably missed a potential opportunity to find out more systemic issues that can be addressed in the system.

Sometimes, even when issues are raised against the process/system rather than the person, it is still very possible to have a conflict. This is why it is very expedient for auditors to agree and explain findings clearly and professionally to auditees at the point when these are identified and to focus wholly on the objective evidence reviewed. Remember that, when you have found a symptom, it might not just be time to establish non-conformity. Try and look for the disease. When you have gathered enough objective evidence of the issue, you should have less resistance, and if there still is resistance, you should follow your company procedure for addressing issues and grievances usually via yours or the auditee's manager.

QUESTION 18

IS THERE ANY RULE THAT REQUIRES US TO SCHEDULE ALL OUR INTERNAL AUDITS WITHIN A CALENDAR YEAR?

The answer is that, according to the ISO 9001 standard, there is *no* such rule.

However, most organisations that are certified to the ISO standard under accreditation requirements by their national accreditation body will usually be expected to have in place an internal audit system that, as a minimum, audits all the requirements of the ISO system within the calendar year.

It is broadly accepted that the calendar year is the convenient, worst-case, timeframe for full internal audits to have been conducted. This might not be unlinked to the standard practice of certification bodies carrying out an annual third party audit of certified organisations.

It is important to note that accredited certification bodies are also subjected to audits, by the accreditation body. In these audits they have to meet a range of requirements of other international standards (other than ISO 9001). And requirements, like the minimum annual full system audits, find their way into certification body procedures to ensure effective system controls; whether or not directly specified by the ISO 9001 standards.

Secondly, while ISO 9001 requirements on internal auditing clause 8.2.2 does not specify timeframes, it states that: '...shall conduct internal audits at planned intervals to determine whether the QMS.... conforms to planned arrangements, to the requirements of this international standard (ISO 9001) and to the QMS requirements established by the organisation...' This requirement requires all parts of the QMS and ISO requirements audited. It only states 'at planned intervals', but once the interval is over the one-year timeframe, it potentially complicates the arrangements.

The most overpowering argument for the one-year maximum timeframe is that it gives a very easily recognisable benchmark timeframe from which reviews and decisions can be made. Sometimes, these longer timeframes are used in organisations that have numerous sites and may be limited, or non-site specific internal audit resources. At the extremes of testing the flexibility of the ISO standard, it might be possible to make a risk-based justification for audit schedules that do not involve a full review of the management system at all operational sites; but it is not best

39

practice and will most likely not be acceptable to your third party certification auditor. As it is their duty to establish continued conformity on a minimum annual basis and an incomplete internal audit, within the stated timeframe, might not provide sufficient evidence to justify continued compliance, the requirement for a minimum annual audit is entrenched in accreditation requirements.

Using a maximum annual rule for the internal audit schedule is of benefit to the organisation, because as a minimum once a year, you can verify that your system is fit for purpose and identify any improvements required. It also assists your company to meet its certification requirements and it probably assists your certification body to successfully justify its accreditation activities. These arguments, for me, justify a schedule that covers the full system on a wider timescale and any related justifications drawn out to it. However, it is possible that there are valid reasons, like distant and difficult to access locations, seasonal operations, and the likes. These would, and should, have been addressed by a plan at your initial certification.

QUESTION 19

INTERNAL AUDITS - WHAT SHOULD DETERMINE THE QUALITY AND QUANTITY OF THE AUDIT REPORT?

There is a quantity of audit report that is called 'too little'. If you have carried out an audit for half a day and you have a report that is less than a page, it would be considered too small. A rule of thumb to use is to look at your audit report and answer the following questions

1. Does it detail the objective evidence reviewed during the audit?

2. Is it a fair reflection of the time spent carrying out the audit i.e. half a page for a half day audit will likely be below expectations

3. Does it demonstrate that I have been professional in doing my audit? Remember professionalism here refers to good objective evidence, optimal use of time and your report being a document that can be used for any future reference.

It is important to note that some internal audit arrangements are structured for very minimal report writing and some are simple tick box checklists. Without going on to what is a different question, whatever the methodology you use, documenting adequate objective evidence of samples seen, documents reviewed, personnel interviewed, other evidence reviewed is important to putting together a good report.

Many audit reports contain statements such as 'the process for the control of records is effective'. That is more like a conclusion than audit evidence. This kind of statement would be expected in the summary. Before you can come to this conclusion you must have 'tested' the efficacy of the arrangements for the control of records. You must have looked for or requested some specific records, verified they were well stored and easily retrievable; verified they were legible and arrangements were in place to keep them up to the timescales defined by the management system.

As a rule of thumb I pick five or six random samples for most audits- you could choose more or less. You want to document these samples. Let's say you choose 10 samples; you might decide not to put down the details of all the samples you chose, but you want to document enough sample evidence to justify any conclusions that you come to. I have established

41

this at about five or six for many simple processes in my own audits. But of course audit sampling should be done relative to the risks and sample size available. Audit sampling is not documented in any sample plan tables; there is a softer edge to audit sampling that relies on the judgement of the auditor.

If the audit report is looking like a piece of prose, you are probably not recording the right things. An audit report should be peppered with document names, numbers and identification, personnel names, dates, quantities, descriptions, event times, numbers, locations, equipment identification etc. because it is all about objective evidence. I believe the ultimate test for a good audit report is if it can be picked up 12 months from the date it was written by an independent person and the person can successfully retrieve and verify all objective evidence detailed in the report; then that report is likely to have been clearly written and laid out. Remember that the audit report is not intended as a document owned by the auditor, it is for the purpose of management and any interested stakeholders to review the basis of any conclusions drawn.

QUESTION 20

HOW WILL THE REQUIREMENT FOR RISK BASED THINKING AFFECT INTERNAL AUDITS IN THE NEW STANDARD ISO9001:2015?

In many ways this question on its own sits slightly in uncharted waters, and should formulate itself over time. The following is a fundamental theory of what is expected to happen:

1. Firstly internal auditors will need to have an understanding of the specific risks of the business and the process of the areas that are under audit. It does not necessarily have to be a deep understanding but an understanding of the potential risks associated with that particular area.

2. Internal auditors will have to begin to make use of risk based planning and scheduling of their audits. If for example, some departments have greater risk exposure than others, it might make sense for the auditor to audit the more risk-exposed departments more frequently than those with less risk exposure.

An example would be a legal firm that receives clients' original documents, scans them and sends them back. In this case the control and record of documents will take on a totally new significance in the scanning function of the business. Of course the law in regards to people's personal data will have to be looked into, ensuring that information is accessible, well labeled and returned as agreed. You might want to audit the document control process of clients' original documents to a greater depth than you might do on document control process in the warehouse area. This is also because you would audit those processes in the warehouse, which have higher significance than the document control process.

3. There has to be risk-based action. Risk-based action can

43

vary and is dependent on the system, it can be based on timelines for corrective actions pending, critically weighting, whether major or minor non-conformity, and even scaling up if issues of particular descriptions need to be scaled up.

These are some of the things that, in my opinion, will change in the way internal audits are carried out in regards to risk.

The core processes are expected to have more audit time and frequency, probably more than the supporting processes. But this judgment will be based on an understanding of the particular risk, not just of that process, but of the business that is being audited or the particular areas that are being audited. Sometimes the planning would be a function of previously identified risks. If you have had some recurring issues that have been happening regularly then they could rise in risk rating which means you focus on them more than others. A good example here, assuming that the company in question has international operations, is that the international operation might be more

exposed to risk. This is because as an international company it will have less control over the international operation than those where your base may be located. Therefore, you might want to audit the international operations in more detail especially if there are some requirements for additional compliance, over which it might be difficult to monitor. You will need people outside of your immediate organisation or the core QMS skill set within your own location and rely on them to carry out those functions. A variety of factors will determine the risk profile of the company and many events may change that risk profile from time to time. Internal auditors will have to increase their knowledge and understanding of ever changing risk profiles and be able to adapt to these changes.

Some organisations have been carrying out risk based auditing in a variety of ways but it is hoped that it will be a more holistic approach and there will be a requirement for every organisation to demonstrate that risk based approach even within their own internal audit system. This is the intent of the ISO9001:2015 standard.

BONUS ISO 9001:2015 QUESTIONS

WE KNOW THAT ONE OF THE KEY CHANGES IN THE 2015 VERSION IS FOR DETAILED REQUIREMENTS ON THE LEADERSHIP, BEING MORE PARTICIPATIVE AND LEADING THE QUALITY MANAGEMENT SYSTEM. HOW WILL WE AUDIT THIS? MORE IMPORTANTLY HOW WILL WE RAISE NON-CONFORMITY WITH, MAYBE EVEN MY BOSS'S BOSS, AS AN INTERNAL AUDITOR?

ISO9001 has always had a number of criticisms; one being that its requirements are difficult for small, medium size and micro businesses to fulfil. However, having this new requirement for leadership (which is a strengthening of management responsibility), might make it easier for small and medium sized businesses to comply with than the big corporations. In many ways by the nature of SMEs, senior management is hands on and involved in the QMS, maybe even carrying out internal audits, pushing them forward and getting all their employees to do what they need to do with regard to quality. If they already have a structured management system with the 2008 version and they are able to demonstrate that leadership is being championed across the board, it might be a lot easier to fulfil that requirement.

From an internal auditors' perspective, how do I audit the boss? There are some simple methods already being used such as management reviews and whether actions arising from management reviews are being carried out. Look at audits internally and external, especially if they require senior management involvement or resources from senior management and how engaged they were with the process of getting that rectified. Find evidence of senior management effectively championing the management system. Typically you will always have a senior management signature on the quality policy but what other things are on the notice board? Is it only the management representative that is involved in much of these communications and driving initiatives? In many ways what used to be the role of management representative, is now changing in that you want senior management to now be fulfilling a significant part of that role. These are the kind of evidences you are looking for but they less tangible than others.

If you actually have to directly interview senior management, I would suggest that this is the last part of the audit, having already collected information from other parts of the business, such as management reviews, status of conformity process, quality policy, quality objectives, etc. Coming to that interview where the findings can be put across to senior management so it becomes more of a measurement of their awareness and understanding of the issues that are at stake. It is their involvement and concern with getting solutions to these issues, which will give a clearer picture of what we are trying to achieve; which is to assess the engagement of senior management involvement in quality management systems and their related processes.

It might be a softer audit to begin with but when you put together the range of objective evidence that has been found prior to sharing with management, then you can make a judgement or assessment based on objective evidence of, for example, how many actions have been closed from previous management reviews or how many requests for resources have been fulfilled or how many engagements senior management has had with the team.

In regard to the second question about raising a non-conformity against

the boss's boss (employer). This will totally depend on the culture of the organisation, it could be a very bad idea to raise non-conformity against the boss and then get fired. If the organisation is not responsive, any reasonable internal or external auditor will be satisfied with objective evidence of some of these issues which we have talked about. This has to be very objective; it cannot be simply a grudge because management has gone against the wishes or needs of your department. In this case, no one including ISO will back the individual when they get fired.

Always stick to objective evidence, particularly in the case of auditing senior management. Objective evidence will always mean documentation and verifiable evidences. Word of mouth is very weak objective evidence; in actual fact some auditors do not consider it as objective evidence at all. If there are fundamental issues that cannot be raised without causing problems with the employer, it might be in the internal auditor's best interest to wait for an external auditor to pick this up.

Note: This is said knowing that most readers are from small or medium size businesses, in which case they might be close enough to senior management not be to able to effectively maintain objectivity through this process, which is why this advice is given.

If the culture of the business allows, then go ahead and do what needs to be done. Always remain professional and stick to the objective evidence. Remain wise as, knowledge is knowing what to say, but wisdom is knowing when and how to say it.

BONUS ISO 9001:2015 QUESTIONS

ISO9001:2015 REMOVES THE REQUIREMENT FOR DOCUMENTS AND RECORDS WILL THIS MEAN THAT WE CAN CARRY OUT AN INTERNAL AUDIT WITHOUT AN AUDIT REPORT?

The standard removes the expression 'documents and records', but brings in the expression, 'documented information'. Documents and records are included in the definition of documented information, but the definition becomes broader because it will cover other forms of evidences such as new media, apps, videos, etc. It, therefore, does not remove the requirement for documents and records; it rather includes it within the context of a wider way of demonstrating it.

In the new standard, one will notice that there is a continued use of the word 'evidenced' and 'documented information'. For many small, medium and micro businesses, the access to all these other sophisticated means of evidencing compliance may not be readily available. Where you don't have evidences such as apps, software systems, videos, CCTV (Closed Circuit Television) evidence, etc. to support what you need to prove for your quality system, it would be better to stick to good old records and documents to verify processes.

The job of the internal audit is to verify that these things work and when an external auditor wants to verify that an internal audit process is in place then he wants to see the evidence of your internal audit. One of the applications seen more recently is where audits are being carried out relatively remotely, which means that the auditor does not have to go and see each person at a time. In this case they would just send a list of questions and information requests to various members of the business, who fill in all this online, which the auditor reviews at the back end. This may not necessarily have a written auditor report but it might just be a combination of various reports that have come in from various people within the organisation. This is classified as evidence; there is a broad perception of what can be evidence in the light of the modern system that the standard is trying to bring in. Unless the use of something overtly sophisticated is in place, records and documents should still be used for internal audits, except where there are other clear ways of showing evidence. For example if you video your entire audit process, that is good evidence. The organisation would not

48

be penalised for not complying with the requirements of carrying out internal audits for having video evidence.

This does not remove the requirement to have an audit report but it widens the ways in which the internal audit carried out can be demonstrated. Where those sophisticated tools are not available one of the easiest ways and most common ways of still demonstrating or evidencing things is documents and records, records of that internal audit will be acceptable evidence under the requirements of the new standard.

It is recognised that the focus of this Book is on internal audits but one of the skills that internal auditors have to get to grips with is a full understanding of the requirements of the 2015 version and the interpretation of that. Whatever is written in the 2015 version does not negate the foundational audit requirement of obtaining objective evidence. Where organisations interpret or misinterpret the removal of words, documents and records for not having things evidenced, then the internal auditor has the duty of finding as much available evidence as possible to demonstrate compliance with whatever process is actually being audited. Organisations need to obtain objective evidence. This requirement is not negated in the new standard.

ACKNOWLEDGEMENT

Writing a book, even a small one like this is a demanding task. First I want to thank everyone that sent in a question when I sent out the request and indeed everyone who has inspired some questions and perhaps the answers here by virtue of learning and experiences I have gained by coming in contact with them in the course of my career in Quality.

My thanks to Gregory H Watson, past president of the International Academy for Quality, recipient of several awards in the quality profession and one of the foremost thought leaders in the Quality profession in the world today, for taking the time to review this piece and his feedback and comments. I am very honoured and very grateful.

I will also like to appreciate our small but mighty team at Charis Management Systems, everyone playing their distinctive role in the company. Special thanks to Chiko Chupa, our Projects Executive who helped to get on paper some of the materials from audio when putting down the last few chapters was taking longer than scheduled; I guess they call it a writer's block!

Finally to my home team, my wife Shimona and sons 'Bomi and 'Shomi. Thanks for the many hours you freed up for me to get this little project done.

'Yemi

October 2015

www.ingramcontent.com/pod-product-compliance
Lightning Source LLC
Chambersburg PA
CBHW071336200326
41520CB00013B/3003